The Season of Reason

By

Mungoni Manoge

© PJ NTSOANE

Give a Read Gift

© PJ NTSOANE
PO BOX 941
LEBOWAKGOMO
POLOKWANE
LIMPOPO PROVINCE
RSA
0737

First Published in 2014

© All rights reserved. No part of this publication may be reproduced, stored in a retrieval system, or transmitted in any form or by any means, electronic, mechanical, photocopying, recording, or otherwise without either the prior written permission of the publisher or a license permitting restricted copying.

Cover Artwork by Marcus

ISBN: 978-0-620-63175-4

©PJ NTSOANE

Mungoni Manoge

About the author

Mungoni Manoge is a pen name used by Photoane Jeffrey Ntsoane. It echoes the name of his tribe Bakone ba Manoge who are part of the Bakone (baKoni) tribes found in the northern parts of the Republic of South Africa. Oral history says that they are the same family as the amaNguni in Southern Africa and Angoni in Central Africa.

NB: Mungoni Manoge is opposed to tribalism, racism and gender discrimination.

Contents

1. My Eyeballs
2. Politics
3. To the Dictator
4. The Puppets
5. In Cahoots
6. Big Head
7. True Love
8. United We Stand
9. Nepotism
10. Prejudice
11. To the Rescue
12. A Thought Cloud
13. My Blackberry
14. A True Corner Stone
15. Go Get It.
16. Political Power
17. What Do We Have?
18. Revolution
19. Flower Power
20. Naturally Fantastic
21. Hazy Day

©PJ NTSOANE

22. Learning
23. Anger in the neighbourhood
24. I Lie Awake
25. The Poor's Lament
26. Lord Have Mercy
27. The Careless
28. Dr Medication
29. One Night Stand
30. The Herd Boys
31. The Bug
32. In the Moonlight
33. Graduation
34. Addiction
35. I am no loafer
36. Democracy
37. Better off
38. This World is going down
39. Expectation
40. She Ran off
41. On Your Own
42. Keep the Faith
43. The Poor

©PJ NTSOANE

44. The People's government
45. Why me?
46. The Shopping Mall.
47. Let Me Confess
48. Step by Step
49. Political Ladder
50. Thirsty
51. Haunter

1. My Eyeballs

My eyeballs feed me with your beauty;
Feebly I ogle and salivate so much I feel guilty,
Yours is beauty seldom seen in this world,
No wonder my mind is running wild.

The Lord's commandment says I shouldn't covet;
I am caught hard and tight like a horn in a net;
Before my God I fall and confess my sin,
I ask for forgiveness as I am burning deep within.

Will you rescue me from this suffering?
I am as hapless as a lamb tied for offering;
I have vainly tried to wriggle free,
In essence I am bound like a prisoner would be.

My heart is beating in the rhythm of your name,
Let me diamond your finger to lay my claim.

©PJ NTSOANE

2. Politics

Politics sucks like ticks,
That's when politicians play their dirty tricks.
They would lay snares for their opponents,
They become as useless as pipes with open ends.

Politicians' delivery of the desired aims is leaky;
That is when the game field becomes freaky;
Then the rules of the game are always flouted,
People's aims and goal posts become clouded.

The referee's whistle is muzzled;
The state's resources are unevenly parcelled;
Only the network receives the signal,
As always, the circle's words are final.

When you dare beep a protest,
You are blamed for not being modest.
That formerly fair and friendly democracy,
Its essence is ghastly like a demon gone crazy.

Those doors which were once wide open,
Painted guards, slam them to the orphan.
The nation's means serve the interest of the few,
The blindfolded members of the crew!

©PJ NTSOANE

3. To the Dictator

Who gave you the right to sit in that parliament?
Whoever is responsible knows how to tease;
To the conscious your rule is pure lament,
You are allergic to the word peace.

The wailing of the just is music to your ears;
Every day you easily produce a martyr;
You are the top waster of your peers,
I wonder how many more you will murder.

Your smile mirrors a grimace;
Your foul smell can be sensed many miles away,
Shrewdness is written all over your face,
Your wicked whim always holds sway.

Like tornado your will blows up our conscience,
You make common people lose common sense.

©PJ NTSOANE

4. The Puppets

Ever seen the puppets made to buy a pup?
A tornado is sold to them as a storm in a cup,
The master likes it only when they are in a nap,
He knows they will blindly fall into a trap.

Conniving spiders spin their silky web;
The con artist is moving like a crab in the ebb,
The empty head shells are multiplied,
Just like pied birds they are tied.

The simple head is the master's gain;
His sack is always full of grain;
The puppet has no spine,
Wherever the master pulls his strings it is fine.

The puppets move involuntarily,
They stop as the mover stops momentarily.

©PJ NTSOANE

5. In Cahoots

Those in cahoots are as fragile as plant shoots;
They sell one size fits-all boots,
But one slip of a babbling chatter-box,
Without coaxing there is a spanner in the cogs.

Enjoy cahoots shine while it lasts,
It will soon snap like sail on old masts!
There is time for everything,
One bright day the culprits will also get a sting,

Hopefully you will be allergic;
We would like to see reality play its comic;
Let the misled wallow in laughter!
The parent should join the son and daughter,

Their long awaited lovely day has arrived,
This ending is self-contrived.

©PJ NTSOANE

6. Big Head

Yours is a mountain of a head;
No wonder it is as heavy as lead;
Your neck is as succulent as a baby stem,
Your empty ego is fired by the wayward system.

Your short-sightedness makes you blind;
You cannot see beyond the horizon grind,
Enjoy the fake moments while they last!
You should know the fallen blasts from the past!

Many succumbed to complacency;
They trivialised urgency;
They thought the world was their oyster,
Now even their skin has lost its moisture.

You are following the same foot-path,
Therefore you are risking God's wrath.

©PJ NTSOANE

7. True Love

True love is eternal;
In the rhythm of the heart it is a signal;
True love glitters forever like diamonds,
The names of true lovers are in Heavenly fonts.

The mark of love lingers more than a tattoo;
True love cages you like an animal in the zoo;
One who is love drunk entertains world eyes,
All that should be a definite: No, is a loud: Yes!

You become head over heels,
Your head reels;
The images of the loved fill lovers' minds,
The loved one's absence absolutely grinds.

True love conquers all!
Even big empires are weakened to fall.

©PJ NTSOANE

8. United we stand

United we can win!
We can give this round world a good spin;
United we are unbreakable like a bundle,
To our foes we will be too hot to handle!

Don't search for flaws to spite your comrade;
Yet for the course call a spade a spade!
Spur your comrades to give their all,
Shun working hard for one another's fall!

Your comrade's flaw may be your own demise;
Don't hand your enemy the winner's prize!
There is no chain stronger than its weakest link,
In the deep blue sea let's not make our ship sink.

United let's stand,
With our lives let's defend our brand!

©PJ NTSOANE

9. Nepotism

We all know that blood is thicker than water,
But at the nation's cost it's a serious matter.
Take care of your loved ones with own expenses!
That will be sweet to our human senses.

We entrusted you with our resources;
You thank us with your corrupt forces,
How could you become parasitically greedy?
You turn a deaf ear to the cries of the needy.

A true leader thinks about the people;
That's when success will permeate with a ripple;
Everyone will wear a smiling face,
Your name will not become a disgrace.

You have the right to take care of your own,
But be careful not to make the nation frown.

©PJ NTSOANE

10. Prejudice

Prejudice is ire like an incurable disease;
The sufferers do not know peace,
The blindfolded become naïve to reality,
Like a drug they are victims amenable to cruelty.

Your bile churns a lush soil for the seeds of hate;
The prejudiced enjoy the meal on racist plate;
The tummy is filled with the acrid,
The mouth spews lethal acid.

All that you need is to make the victim suffer;
The twisted mind urges your mouth to say *kaffir*,
Unawares you stoop to the level of a pig,
You wallow in the mud and think you are big.

Please read the right page,
You'll know that God created man in His image.

©PJ NTSOANE

11. To the rescue

We are stranded out here in the deep blue sea;
Like timid and confused crew we flee;
Every man desires to save own skin,
We all have own hearts beating within.

We forget about doing justice unto others;
Another man's plea for mercy bothers,
A call to the rescue goes unheeded,
Survival tricks are the most needed.

We are longing for the reality of superman;
Yes, we are doing the best we can!
Yet our best seems to be wanting,
With utter desperation we are panting.

It is time to cast our eyes to Heaven,
Only with God's help we can break even.

©PJ NTSOANE

12. A Thought Cloud

If we had a thought cloud hanging over us;
We would not worry about the cheating fuss,
No one would make us believe their rotten lies,
We would not be fooled by faking eyes.

No one would give an empty promise;
We would see that something was amiss;
Governments would have clean members,
No spin doctor for what everyone remembers.

No wife would have a tears-drenched pillow;
Lovers would grow in abundance like a willow,
Happiness would flourish every day,
The playground would be adorned with fair play.

Spears would be too blunt for backstabbing,
There would be no news that is disturbing.

©PJ NTSOANE

13. My Black Berry

Hello, my beautiful country black berry!
Crossing the channels to you I need no ferry;
You look so fresh and smooth,
This heart's longing ache is for you to sooth.

Your sweetness is beyond comparison;
I am forever hooked to you for a reason;
You have the sweetest juice in the whole world,
My life without you would be weird.

Your blackness is tantalizing in the sunshine;
I will do anything for you to be mine;
You tickle my taste buds like no other,
I will come to you even in the worst weather.

You are my African beauty,
My lips will always call you sweetie.

©PJ NTSOANE

14. A True Corner Stone

I came and knocked on your door;
I asked you to afford me just one night shelter,
Even if it meant sleeping on the floor,
You tip-toed helter-skelter,
Then you slammed the door in my face!
You kicked me out into the chilly night;
You called me a nonentity and a disgrace;
You took away my only light.

You yelled that you weren't related to low lives!
You were my only hope;
Since you were blessed with bee hives,
But unawares you made yourself a long rope.

Now you are all poor and alone,
Like builders you refused a true corner stone.

©PJ NTSOANE

15. Go Get It.

If you want to achieve a goal,
Go get it and free your soul!
No matter how rock hard it may seem,
Reaching your dream is tastier than a rich cream.

You will make many enemies on the road;
You don't have to discard the heavy load;
When you meet obstacles on the way,
Do anything but don't stray!

You mustn't let your train go off the rails!
Swim like a whale and put up your sails!
Ride the high tide,
Develop the tenacity of a hide!

Fix your eyes on the big prize,
Do not listen to the foes' lies!

©PJ NTSOANE

16. Political Power

Although political power is not eternal,
Political acts are indelible;
In our minds' archives they are forever visible,
The fall of great empires is always phenomenal.

When the captives' chains are finally broken;
The oppressor's head is held as trophy token;
The chickens have come home to roast,
The victorious raise their glasses in a toast.

The writing had always been on the wall;
Your empty head judged the bound as small;
Their grieving cries fell on deaf ears,
You used to wring their eyes of tears.

Power has evaporated like dew at sunrise,
Your forces were taken by surprise.

©PJ NTSOANE

17. What Do We Have?

Deep in the midst of concrete and steel jungle,
Hungry brown flowers adorn the forlorn streets,
The downtrodden beg alms in a mumble,
The grass-tops' fingertips itch for twits.

Here blood is lighter than water;
Name dropping is all the rage;
One's bank balance is the main matter,
Only the connected read from the same page.

The grass-roots can only afford the aroma;
Only eyes can afford beyond the bare necessities,
It appears that their luck goddess is in a coma,
When the Sun sets it ushers in harsh realities.

What have we to offer?
When shall the poor cease to suffer?

©PJ NTSOANE

18. Revolution

We need a revolution for evolution!
To some the word breeds revulsion;
Others pay the ultimate price,
It is the transaction for freedom spice.

The one who reaps in the status quo despairs,
He dreads a long fall down the stairs;
When the oppressed march to freedom square,
We know it is stage time for the people's choir.

Revolution marks the end of the old system;
It is the advent of the new anthem;
Let us forgive but not forget the past vile,
Together hand in hand we can go the extra mile.

Let the revolution shear the old fur,
Let the born-frees enjoy the fanfare.

©PJ NTSOANE

19. Flower Power

Your beauty excites my aesthetic senses;
The power of your attraction overwhelms;
My resistance is devoid of its defences,
I thank God for the benevolence of your stems,

Stretch your pretty arms you natural wonder!
Continue to give your sweet gift!
Let your presence be felt here and yonder,
Only you give my senses a lift!

I adore your velvety touch;
Suffer me to flaunt you to all,
You are my precious catch,
That is the reason why I walk tall.

Holding you is a miracle,
I thank God for your oracle.

20. Naturally Fantastic

There is no flower that smells sweeter than you;
In my eyes your beauty will endlessly endure;
Your eyes will forever ignite the fire in my heart,
No human effort will ever make me depart!

I pray that your pronouncements be for keeps;
Your broom is always the only one that sweeps,
Your face will never be a waterfall,
So long as your territory is under my call.

Do not ever worry about tomorrow;
No weed will ever grow in our furrow,
Life will be as cool as cucumber,
Your sweetness will never make me slumber.

Do not worry about going plastic!
You are naturally terrific.

21. A Hazy Day

Let us give ourselves a brace;
People are disappearing without a trace,
Let us rub our eyes to see,
Dig up the reason the people flee!

Let us stretch and sketch the horizon!
We need to figure out how to stop the crimson;
We need to find our way on this hazy day,
Let our children run around and play!

Why is the neighbourhood amok?
Let the elders stop and take stock!
Ask the Lord to remove the heavy load!
Ask Him to clear obstacles on the road!

Switch on the headlights!
We need to see the road out of the dark nights.

©PJ NTSOANE

22. Learning

Like a typewriter printing on a sheet,
The mind gets blotted with information.
Like a new-born cub wobbling on its feet,
The children saunter in education.
Like the stray in the wilderness,
They are groping in stark darkness.

There is grabbing and standing on thin ice;
Some manage to win the first price;
Like manna hope is tumbling down,
Old men are still searching for life of their own,
There is light at the end of the tunnel,
Success poured comes in through tight funnel.

The dogs are fighting for the lone bone,
Injustice is justice in the eyes of the clone.

©PJ NTSOANE

23. Anger in the neighbourhood

There rolls the drum beat!
The people dance and gasp for air;
The wide windows cannot cool the heat,
In the concrete jungle the lost lambs blare.

A swift cold breeze blasts from the South;
Absent mothers and fathers don't come forth,
The tall and the short,

The big and the small,
The lean and the stout,
All never heed the young's call.

Sham smiles on the faces;
There is celebration of empty unity of races;
Paradox of iniquity for the have-nots,
That is the reason the ostrich's head nods.

©PJ NTSOANE

24. I Lie Awake

I lie awake all night,
For me nothing seems all right,
I sleep in a river of tears,
I only have a bitter splash of torrents for cheers.

I have a log to hold on to,
That is all I can do,
My arms long for a warm hug,
Instead I fall into a bottomless pit ever dug.

My trembling hands hold on for dear life;
I grab the sharp edge of the knife,
I hopelessly pretend,
Blindfolded I see vividly everything decent.

I try hard to enjoy the game,
Everyone can see it is not the same.

©PJ NTSOANE

25. The Poor's Lament

I saw you giving me a despising look;
You force a smile like a frustrated cook;
You look at me askance,
You never give the likes of me a slim chance.

You wallow in mire of fear,
Your wealth disfigures you with a sneer.
Why don't you feel for the needy?
Why don't you take leave from being greedy?

Will you ever do something good?
I am on all fours begging for food,
I know it is all yours,
That is why I am begging by force.

If you give a little hand out,
You can save the crowd.

26. Lord Have Mercy

Only the bloodthirsty got fed on this bloodshed;
Lord have mercy, it is making the children sad!
The rivers of blood flow from every direction,
They flow into the sea of destruction,
That is the never filled vampire's belly,
We have to go clean the streams in the valley!

The East is red as it is daybreak;
The forces of doom fight without a break;
All day long until the Sun goes down in the West,
During the night the good is brought to waste,
The guns roar like fire crackers until morning,
The families start with their routine mourning.

Many love to talk about peace on earth,
Yet they give you a kiss of death.

©PJ NTSOANE

27. The Careless

I like to steal a glimpse of you;
That I enjoy the sight of you is true,
I follow you wherever you go,
I like it when you bend down low.

I cannot help it but stare,
Whenever you carelessly bare,
The beauty of the sight I see is untold,
I am moved whenever I catch that fleeting gold.

The ten seconds moment of wealth fades away;
I thank Heavens for enriching me a bit anyway;
I pray that Heavens lose an angel again,
For that is when all my troubles wane.

The careless thief disturbs my dream,
Why wake me up when I don't scream?

©PJ NTSOANE

28. Dr Medication

I call upon you Dr Medication;
Please hand in your solution!
I am in need of your help,
My health is in ebb,
Break these pains of demonic chain!
Again let me wade through the pleasure plain!

It is long that I have been down;
Someone has long been wearing my crown;
I have been suffering from this heat,
My children want to dance to the drum beat,
Their eyes have become dry,
As there are no more tears to cry.

Help me remove this servitude stain,
So I can lock hands with my loved ones again.

©PJ NTSOANE

29. One Night Stand

It was here when we went to sleep;
It was no more when the dawn came;
Some things we cannot keep,
It is a take, lick and discard game.

It enlivened the night time;
It was so close to the skin,
Yet it vanished in its prime,
It made our heads spin.

I want to set the record straight;
Do not close the gate!
You may call it one night stand,
Please call again, you sweetest brand.

A brief love song to sing,
Let us give it one more swing!
When the time comes we shed no tears,
We bury it as it wasn't meant to last for years.

©PJ NTSOANE

30. The Herd Boys

In the morning dew we milk the cows;
When we hear the sound of the crows;
It is time to head to the forest,
Where the lions roar and rest,
We look after our father's cattle,
We fight the mock warrior battle.

We play our hunting games;
We learn the jungle names;
We make sure the cattle don't stray,
We keep the predators and thieves at bay.
Birds praise us with their sweet songs;
Game stampede in their throngs;
Thunder rolls in the distance,
The lions roar in assistance.

When we see birds returning to their nests;
Maidens begin prancing to entertain guests;
We know it is time to return home,
We retire to our father's warm fire dome.

©PJ NTSOANE

31. The Bug

I was sitting alone in the dark;
Listening to the song of a skylark;
When I felt a strange sensation,
It was the feeling of passion.

It was fascinating and intoxicating;
The itching made me go twisting;
I longed for your warm hug,
I was sweet-bitterly bitten by a love bug.

It makes me shiver with fever;
I am sweetly infected forever;
I admit that I am in big trouble,
It is so huge it makes me tremble!

I don't want antibodies,
I want us to be more than buddies.

©PJ NTSOANE

32. In the Moonlight

The air is as fresh as juicy fruit;
All the jokes suit the birthday suit,
We are walking hand in hand in the sand,
Our eyes are fed by the view of the land.

The touches so sweet and fresh;
We get caresses from the tidal splash;
Now you and I enjoy the sweet breeze,
Our faces know no anger crease.

The swashing healing sound;
The pulse of our feet firmly on the ground;
We withstand the strongest gale,
The pessimist is painted pale.

Ours is love heartfelt,
Our names will always be well spelt.

©PJ NTSOANE

33. Graduation

It was muscle tearing climbing up rocky surface;
Salty sweat was gushing down your face;
The higher you clung the colder it became,
At dizzy heights you had rock eagles to tame.

The coldness numbed your bony fingers;
You painstakingly put on blinkers,
Your eyes were set on the golden prize,
To overcome obstacles you became wise.

The load was full of inviting off-ramps;
Your legs were assailed by cramps;
There were calls for you to give up,
You refused to be dwarfed like a shrub.

You refused point blank to submit,
Now enjoy the view from the summit!

©PJ NTSOANE

34. Addiction

Addiction is an affliction;
It is like living inside a frying pan,
You only have painful connection,
You are caught in the morass of Satan's plan.

Your life is posted outside your body;
You become a slave and a puppet in one;
You have no sense of being clean or shoddy,
It is a game that is only painfully won.

The chains of hell tie and tear your skin;
Like a coward you sell your soul;
Your life is trapped in the dustbin,
You eternally wallow in a furnace of coal.

Salvation is only in the Word,
By the Word the world was created by the Lord.

©PJ NTSOANE

35. I'm no Loafer

Stop calling me a loafer!
You pierce my heart with a spear;
I have searched the town all over,
Stop hitting me with your prickly pear!

I spent sleepless nights,
I read and wrote,
I thought that would take me to dizzy heights;
But in the mailbox I find eviction note;
I happen to be the unfortunate beggar,
It seems I am condemned to do no better,
If circumstances prevail many will be wailing,
Only a few members of the crew will be sailing.

Many still hit the bedrock;
All they hear will be prison lock,
If the wind were to change the course,
Many will be a robust force.

©PJ NTSOANE

36. Democracy

Come fold up the sleeves of your brands!
We need to muddy our hands;
Let us lay the bricks and mortar of democracy!
There is no place for the lazy.

Africa my home continent,
We know colonialism left a dent.
Let us do what is right,
We need to chase away darkness with the light!

The young and old fill up the emptiness!
Let us make it our everyday business!
What is the use of racism?
Why do you hide behind tribalism?
All they can churn out is strife,
There is no need to draw out your knife.

We do not need to sow the seed of animosity;
We do not need the crop of agony;
Let us not have unnecessary blisters,
We are all brothers and sisters.

©PJ NTSOANE

37. Better off

You are as heavy as lead;
I thought I would fly like a bird;
But with you on my back,
I have totally lost my track.

I always thought you were light,
How I misjudged your weight?
I have always regarded myself as ox-strong,
Now I know how I was wrong.

Like a broken ship in a storm I sink;
Sorry to admit I couldn't think;
The passage is too small for both of us,
If ever we are going to pass

We need to go it alone!
It is better than watering a stone.

©PJ NTSOANE

38. This World is going down

I was in my shelter one night;
I saw a man in disguise;
I couldn't make out his exact height,
He had piercing red fiery eyes.

I stood there in a frozen startle;
I nervously looked around,
His brazen voice rang out: 'Battle!'
Then I saw children lying on the ground.

They had had overdose rammed up their noses;
They face shrapnel danger every day;
Their little hearts desired fresh roses,
But someone's greed denied them their play.

The world has rising flood;
It is raining bombs and blood,
Indoctrination,
Starvation,
Bigotry,
Cruelty,
Crime,
Slime,
Illusion,
And pollution!
This white, blue, black and brown,

©PJ NTSOANE

This World is going down!

39. Expectation

I am waiting for you to come;
This game is doing me great harm,
I am so restless,
My life is a mess!

My eyes are fixed at one direction;
Your love is my only predilection;
The time is tickling towards the hour,
I am fascinated by your sensational power,
I am so restless lovely.

When will the phone ring?
I am pondering,
When shall I hear your knock?
Please don't make me a laughing stock.

I sent you a message yesterday;
When you said you were coming straight away,
I began to wait in anticipation,
When is your advent at my location?

This is a long and winding expectation,
It fills me with meditation.

©PJ NTSOANE

40. She Ran off

What wrong have I done now?
I wish someone could tell me somehow;
Is it not that everyone reaps what they sow?
I could not believe what I saw.

My sweetheart ran off,
This is no bluff puff;
She ripped my heart and headed north,
Condolences filtered forth.

They say, 'To everything there is a season.'
Now I have found the reason,
I have to stay alive,
I have to survive!
She has the beauty,
She brightens every party,
She is a follow fashion girl,
Beware because she burns like hell.

©PJ NTSOANE

41. On Your Own

You have to learn to stand on your feet!
You have the whole world to beat;
You are on your own,
Multitudes want your crown.

Don't just sit!
You will never know when you are fit;
You may be wobbly when you start,
You have to strengthen your heart!

With the help from Almighty God;
There will be food in your pot!
Don't worry when nobody gives you a nod,
Give your dream all you have got!

God provides for the birds of the sky;
They feed even when they fly;
Do it while you still have a chance,
Never mind the long distance,
Build your own bridge,
Hold fast or fall off the ridge!

©PJ NTSOANE

42. Keep the Faith

We have mountains to climb;
Everyone is prone to be a lost lamb;
There are jackals hungry for meat,
Leopards wear sheep skins to cheat,
Open your eyes and look out for a trap!
Or you will be devoured like a dressed crab.

Keep the Lord's commandments!
He never lets His child laments;
His children never fear death shadow,
For He makes His sheep graze in the meadow.

So do not let Satan make you believe!
That is the only way you will not grieve.
God's Word conquers any strife,
Only in God's Kingdom there is eternal life.

Don't let hypocrites block your way!
Let no temptation carry you away!
God made the Earth,
That is why you have to keep the faith.

©PJ NTSOANE

43. The Poor

Each has a heap of hardships to bear;
Everyone has a harness of suffering to wear;
The hounds can easily follow their sweat spore,
The tongue tastes stale bitterness for the poor.

Sweet life is only a pie in the sky;
The fountain of basic necessities is always dry;
The poor can only do with ego propelled charity,
The opulent dread the revolutionary parity.

The big Book says blessed are the poor;
But how do we survive this torrent downpour?
Our shacks are forever flooded,
The politicians' speeches are sweet worded.

The leaders ram their meaning down our throats;
We become robust oars to propel their boats;
They cross wide rivers to deliver their lies,
The splashing of the high wave muffles our cries.

We've seen thunder storms sweep away hopes;
The master has tightened the servitude ropes;
Thunderstorms have rainbows,
Only the poor's suffering ever grows.

©PJ NTSOANE

Charity is not freedom,
It is only an illusion to the doomed dumb.

44. The People's government

You are the people's government;
There is no need for corruption cover mend;
You represent the will of the people,
How can you be the majority and be feeble?

You listen to the cries of the masses;
You shorten the gap between classes;
You don't care about personal wealth,
All are afforded good health.

People feel safe in their homes,
There is no bandit that freely roams,
No one goes to bed on an empty stomach,
You want to leave a good mark.

You are the people's choice;
That is why you have become our voice;
You are quick to act,
Regardless, you never hide a hideous fact.

Misappropriation of funds is anomaly;
You spit on nepotism by not hiring family;

No member has a finger in the cookie jar,
You truly treat everybody on par.

45. Why Me?

I am always the one, who is denied human rights,
The one who has to be humiliated day and night,
Why am I the one who has to stretch out a hand?
I am the one who is without own land,
I am the one who is suspected of all crimes,
I am the one who bears all the bad times.

Is this running in my veins?
Was I created to receive all the stains?
Why am I the one who has to be sold to slavery?
My forebears displayed untold bravery,
Yet, they were the ones who were colonised?
We are deemed impossible to be harmonised.

Why am I denied the right to choose?
My people are the ones easily labelled loose,
Yet we believe in one God.
We are the ones getting the brutal prod;
The Word taught us to do justice unto others,
Yet we are always the victims of death orders.

We are the ones not to be trusted,

No apology even when the real culprit is busted.
A cry of anguish is our daily bread,
Why do we always have to lay the bed?

Why me?
Lord, when will I be free?

46. The Shopping Mall

I don't love the shopping mall at all!
Why should I?
It hurts me to peep inside the stall;
I do not have the means to buy,
Just like everybody I do have many a need,
Why do mine seem too numerous to meet?
It hurts to see the few flaunt their wealth;
The envy of the unfortunate is their mirth;
I know those who got it fairly;
I know many, who got it at the poor's expense,
They never wake up early,
Yet they have the thickest purse.

Here at the mall pity is foreign,
It is where the twisted egotists' pockets reign.

©PJ NTSOANE

47. Let Me Confess

Let me make a confession,
Your beauty is overwhelming!
My heart bombards me with feelings of passion;
The looks of your eyes and lips are warming;
Therefore I am raising the white flag,
It is a show of my wish to become your prisoner,
I will be the happiest prisoner in your cell,
It will be heaven compared to this wanting hell.

World languages don't have ample adjectives,
I searched but none could best describe you.
I have even tried the strongest of sedatives,
They all failed to make me forget the pretty you.

I have sent prayers to the Heavenly Father,
Say yes, and stop this suffering going further.

©PJ NTSOANE

48. Step by Step

Step by step in sync we will walk;
Hand in hand, feeling the pulses of our tread;
Word for word we savour our love talk,
String by string the fabric of our love we thread.

Onlookers turn their heads and drool,
Beat by beat their hearts pound in envy,
Drop by drop our love juice keeps us cool,
Pound by pound their chests become heavy.

Bit by bit our future tower we build,
Stand by strand we erect our love nest,
Inch by inch we sew up our family quilt,
Day by day our foes put us to the test.

Step by step we progress,
Then step by step we digress.

©PJ NTSOANE

49. Political Ladder

You are on the top rung of the ladder;
You are branded the political leader;
Don't be like many others!
Those who from the top look down;
Those who forget the pillars of their crown,
The leaders who regard the ordinary as fodders!

The ordinary helped you up to upper echelons;
Don't adopt the style of the chameleons,
And change your true colour in order to mingle!
Remember you couldn't do it being single!
You stepped on our heads and shoulders,
You are our servant, listen to our orders!

We are your political ladder's pillars,
Do not send us your cold blooded killers!

©PJ NTSOANE

50. Thirsty

It was on a boiling Thursday,
And I was feeling desert thirsty.
I felt like a thirsty soldier in a trench;
Then I saw your beauty so first,
The cool feeling that would only thirst-quench;
It's fountain freshness that burst my thirst.

The convalescing deep sip I took,
Down my pipe your sweetness travelled,
Then my whole body shook!
There I sweet trembled!
I thank Heavens for the miracle,
It's a taste of sweet revolution so radical.

The hot, dry thirst so painful,
It was defeated by the angel so beautiful.

©PJ NTSOANE

51. Haunter

Why do you haunt me every minute?
Peace in my life is as dead as a dodo,
When I say I loathe you I mean it,
I pray that you and your ilk perish in toto!

Every night I lie with one eye;
I'm wondering about your next move.
I wish I had the best spy money could buy;
I wouldn't worry about bullet proof.

In homes, churches, malls and on the road,
In the air, pipes and the deep blue sea,
You are ready to throw bodies into a moat,
Your presence is like a sting of a flea!

You are a cold blooded criminal,
I cannot wait to find your terminal!

The End

© Copyright Reserved

www.ingramcontent.com/pod-product-compliance
Lightning Source LLC
Chambersburg PA
CBHW061258040426
42444CB00010B/2413